Mala Discovers

MODERN INDIA

by Alexandria Pereira

© 2024 Alexandria Pereira. All rights reserved.

No part of this book may be reproduced, stored in a retrieval system, or transmitted by any means without the written permission of the author.

AuthorHouse™
1663 Liberty Drive
Bloomington, IN 47403
www.authorhouse.com
Phone: 833-262-8899

Because of the dynamic nature of the Internet, any web addresses or links contained in this book may have changed since publication and may no longer be valid. The views expressed in this work are solely those of the author and do not necessarily reflect the views of the publisher, and the publisher hereby disclaims any responsibility for them.

This book is printed on acid-free paper.

ISBN: 979-8-8230-2929-2 (sc)
ISBN: 979-8-8230-2930-8 (hc)
ISBN: 979-8-8230-2931-5 (e)

Library of Congress Control Number: 2024913537

Print information available on the last page.

Published by AuthorHouse 07/25/2024

The Mystery of History Series
India
Book 4 of 4

To my grandma, whose life work was dedicated to children and their pursuit of knowledge.

"Grandma, what are you doing?" asked Mala.

"I have some cotton from the fields around us and I am spinning it into yarn so I can weave a tablecloth," replied Grandma.

"How did you learn how to do that?" asked Mala.

"Our ancestors taught me," replied Grandma.

"Could we learn more about our ancestors and Indian history today?" asked Mala.

"Yes, let's go to the museum and learn about our Indian history today," replied Grandma.

"For thousands of years, the people of India worked hard and worked together. They hunted and farmed for food, built and defended their homes, and traded with many people in many countries. The many sultans and emperors of India built beautiful forts, palaces, and temples and made governments and rules that helped the people learn new things and have new ideas. Then big trading companies like the British East India Company came to India and started making rules about trading. This was hard on the people of India.

"A man named Robert Clive, who worked for the British East India Company, used British soldiers to fight the people of India and take control of more of the trade in India. The British government was angry at Robert Clive and told him to stop. But he told them no and kept fighting," said Grandma.

"Why didn't the British stop him?" asked Mala.

"Because it took a long time for Clive's letter, telling them "NO", to reach Britain. See Britain and India are so far away from each other, and at that time, a message had to be sent in a letter on a ship, which took a long time to reach Britain," said Grandma.

"How sneaky," said Mala.

"When the British received Robert Clive's letter, the British were very angry and sent him another letter telling him to leave India. When that letter reached India, he did leave. When the British Queen Victoria heard what Robert Clive had been doing, she ended the British East India Company.

The British government then tried to work with the Indian kingdoms. Some kingdoms helped the British because they promised to protect them, and some fought the British. But eventually all the kingdoms let the British make the rules about trading in India.

"Trading continued, and Britain made a lot of money. The British people started to learn new things and have new ideas. They called this the Industrial Revolution.

But the people of India had to do the hard work to make the things that made Britain a lot of money. The people of India did not make a lot of money for themselves," said Grandma.
"That must have been hard on our ancestors," said Mala.
"Yes, it was," said Grandma.

"With some of the money the British made, they built railroads and schools in India. The first railroad, which ran from the city of Bombay to the city of Thane, carried things the people of India made to ships to trade. The schools taught some children new things, like words such as *bangle* and *pajamas*. Then the British built more railroads and schools to help the people of India learn to make even more things to trade. The people of India worked hard, but it was still the British who continued to make a lot of money.

"The British didn't treat the people of India very well and made rules that were hard on them. One rule was that no Indian person could make or sell salt," said Grandma.
"But our ancestors used salt every day in the foods they ate," said Mala.
"Yes, but salt made a lot of money for the British and they didn't want to give that up.

So, the British made a government in India and more rules to help the trading continue, and even made their queen, Queen Victoria, the Empress of India. This was hard for the people, and they wanted the British, their Queen, and their rules to leave.

"Many people in India worked hard trying to change the rules and make the British leave. One Indian man, Mohandas Gandhi, learned new ways to change rules while spending time in South Africa. In India he used what he learned, to change the rules about making and selling salt. Then he helped the people of India work better together," said Grandma. "So, our ancestors could make and sell salt again?" asked Mala. "Yes," said Grandma.

"Then two countries in Europe invaded their neighbors, which began a war called World War II. The British government worked hard to defend Britain and help its neighbors. The people of India helped too. They sent things like food, clothing, and blankets, and they even sent some people to help.

After the war the British government needed to work hard to rebuild British cities and help its people. They did not have the time or money to keep a government in India any longer. Slowly the British left India.

"Even though the people of India wanted the British to leave, they did not like what happened next. For many years, there had been a lot of fighting between people in India, mainly about how people were to live their lives. There was a group of people, led by a man named Muhammad Jinnah, who wanted more power over people's lives. So the British took some land from India and gave it to this group to make their own country.

"This new country was then divided into two parts called West Pakistan and East Pakistan. The people of India could choose which country they wanted to live in, India or Pakistan, but they had to choose. The people who stayed or moved to India continued to learn new things and have new ideas.

"The people in East Pakistan worked hard, farming rice and weaving cloth to trade. But the government in West Pakistan took the money from that trade for itself and put soldiers in East Pakistan to keep the people working hard.

So, the Indian army, with the help of the East Pakistani people, fought and defeated the West Pakistani army and made East Pakistan a new country called Bangladesh. The people of Bangladesh continue to work hard, work together, and learn new things.

"When India gained its independence from Britain, the people were able to make their own government and rules. The kind of government they chose is called a democracy. A democracy is when a government and its rules are made by all its people, not just one person. India is the world's largest democracy.

The people elected Jawaharlal Nehru to be the first leader of the new India. A lot of people in India call their country Bharat, a Sanskrit word," said Grandma.
"So why do other people call our country India?" asked Mala.
"Because the name India comes from the Persian word Indus, for the Indus River, where our Harappan ancestors lived many, many years ago.

"The people of India continued to work hard, learn new things, and have new ideas. They made and shared new forms of art, science, math, and technology that helped people all around the world learn and have new ideas of their own.
An Indian man, named Jagadish Chandra Bose, invented wireless communication, and later other people used his ideas to invent cell phones.

"An Indian man, named Hemachandra, discovered the Fibonacci series many, many years before Leonardo Fibonacci, an Italian man, learned the idea. Could Fibonacci have learned this idea from traders who had learned the idea from someone who knew Hemachandra?" asked Grandma.
"I wonder," said Mala. "We will never know," said Grandma.

"Monks in India have been using the ideas of the Pythagorean theorem for many, many years—long before Pythagoras, a Greek man, learned the idea. Could Pythagoras have learned the idea during his many trips to India?" asked Grandma.
"Perhaps," said Mala. "We will never know," said Grandma.

"Grandma, look!" said Mala.

"Yes, that is India's first satellite, *Aryabhata*. It flew around earth and up in space and helped us answer questions about our sun and about using x-rays in space.

Then India sent a spaceship called *Chandrayaan-1* to the moon. It helped people learn about the moon, and answer questions such as 'What is the moon made of?' and 'Is there water on the moon?'

Next India sent a spaceship called *Mangalyaan* to the planet Mars. It took pictures that helped people learn about Mars and let them look out into our solar system farther than we have been able to see before.

"Then India sent another spaceship named *Chandrayaan-2* to the moon. It tried to answer even more questions. Can people live on the moon? Where did the moon come from? What is its ancestor?

"It took pictures of the moon, and from those pictures, people made a map of the moon. *Chandrayaan-2* had special tools that helped people look in areas that were hard to see and found moonquakes, which are like earthquakes on the moon. People learned a lot about the moon and had new ideas," said Grandma.

"Look Grandma, there is its camera," exclaimed Mala.

"The Indian government works hard to make it easier for the people of India to grow and learn new things. India is working to make more jobs for more people, and farmers are growing more food to trade. India will one day be this world's leader in trade, as well as being the largest democracy," said Grandma.

"That will be really good for India," said Mala.

"It sure will be," said Grandma.

"By knowing about our Indian history, we see how our ancestors learned to work together, learn new things, and have new ideas. Perhaps, Mala, when you are a grandma, more people will have learned new things and have new ideas to continue to help our country and the people of India grow," said Grandma.

"Wow, I hope so," said Mala.

India is such a wonderful place. I learned so much about the history of India. I learned where I came from, and about all the amazing things my ancestors have learned and shared, so I could be here today, with you Grandma, learning about the history of India.
Thank you, Grandma," said Mala.
"You are welcome," said Grandma.

Historical Timeline

1707 AD	Maratha State increases its territory.
1730	Sugarcane starts to grow on Indian farms.
1746	The British and French battle over trade with India.
1750	Chess comes to India.
1751	Robert Clive defeats the French and starts the British rule of India.
1757	The sextant is used during sea exploration and on trading voyages.
1784	British government and rules are implemented in India.
1802	The British East India Company controls trade in India.
1803	The Mughal emperor accepts British protection, and the British gain more control over India.
1823	The Anglo-Maratha wars end with British victory.
1833	The British East India Company trade monopoly with India is abolished.
1853	The first railway line in India runs from Bombay to Thane.
1856	Uprisings begin against British rule.
1858	The British government takes control of northern India and forces the Mughal emperor to give up his throne.
1877	Queen Victoria of Great Britain is proclaimed empress of India.
1885	The Indian National Congress is founded and starts campaigns for independence.
1905	A major earthquake in Lahore, India, claims ten thousand lives.
1929	Mahatma Gandhi begins nonviolent protests to push the British out of India.
1947	India achieves independence from British rule. India and Pakistan are partitioned.
1950	India becomes a republic on January 26.

1965	India and Pakistan fight over the Kashmir region.
1975	India launches its first satellite with the help of the USSR.
2008	India sends its first spaceship to the Moon, *Chandrayaan-1*.
2013	India sends its first spaceship to Mars, *Mangalyaan*.
2014	ISRO makes history when India becomes the first country to reach Mars orbit.
2019	India sends another spaceship to the Moon, *Chandrayaan-2*.

Today the people of India continue to grow, learn new things, and have new ideas.

Educational Support Activities

Basic Human Needs
We need food to eat, clothing to keep us warm, and shelter to keep us safe and dry.
We need to socialize to work together.
We need to solve problems so that we can invent and be creative.

Practical Life and Sensorial Foundation
Plant a seed. Make up a song and dance. Take a bath. Why do we do these things?

History
What have we learned about Indian history? Put each person and event on a timeline. Where are we on the timeline?

Geography and Map Work
Find the country of India on a map. Close your eyes. Can you draw a map of India?

Science
Build a boat, and sail it in a tub of water by blowing on it. How long does it take to get from one end to the other?

Botany
Eat a guava, banana, and potato. Have some rice with mangos and milk.

Peace Curriculum
Share what you have learned about the history of India with someone else. Work together to learn more.